Emperor Qin Shihuang's Eternal Terra-cotta Warriors and Horses

—— A Mighty and Valiant Underground Army Over 2,200 Years Back

Managing editor : Li Bing-wu

Compiled by Shaanxi Historical Relics Bureau

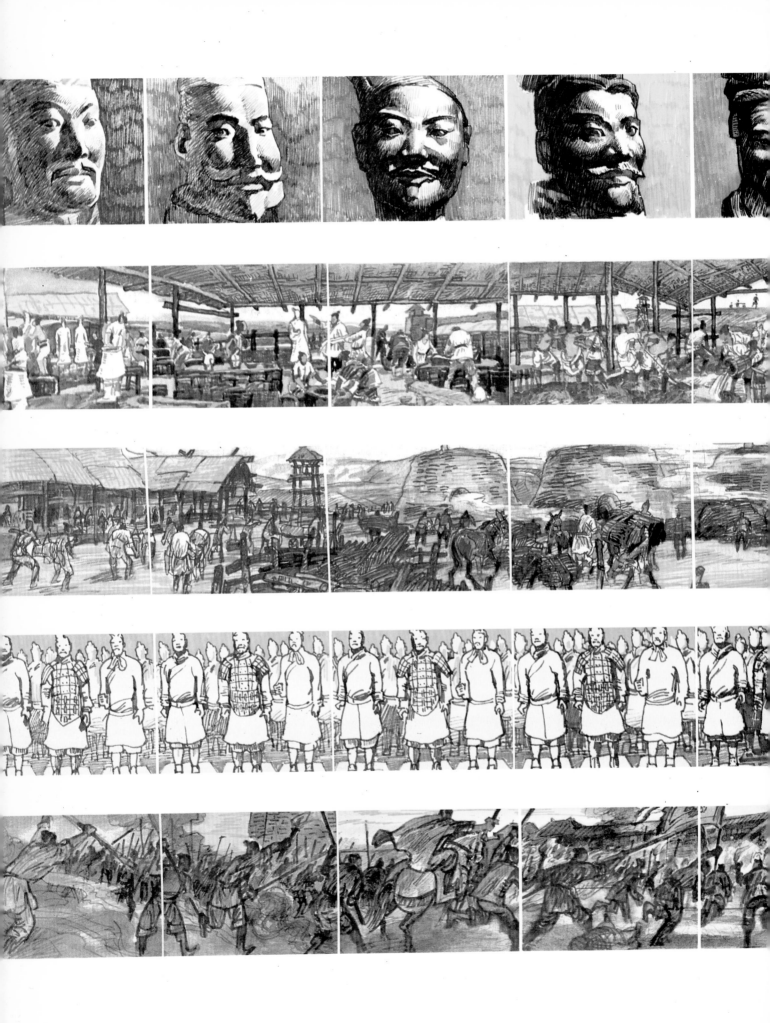

UNITED NATIONS EDUCATIONAL,
SCIENTIFIC AND
CULTURAL ORGANIZATION

CONVENTION CONCERNING THE PROTECTION OF THE WORLD CULTURAL AND NATURAL HERITAGE

*The World Heritage Committee
has inscribed*

The Mausoleum of the First Qin Emperor

on the World Heritage List

*Inscription on this List confirms the exceptional
and universal value of a cultural or
natural site which requires protection for the benefit
of all humanity*

DATE OF INSCRIPTION

11 December 1987

DIRECTOR-GENERAL
OF UNESCO

▲ The Document of the heritage of World Culture by UN

Emperor Qin Shihuang's Eternal Terra—cotta Warriors and Horses
———A Mighty and Valiant Underground Army Over 2,200 Years Back

Table of Contents

● Emperor Qin Shihuang in Profile (1)

● A World—Shaking Discovery (26)

● A Mighty Army in Full Battle Array (44)

● A Statue Complex of High Artistic Value (90)

● The Exquisite Weaponry of the Qin Dynasty (105)

● Emperor Qin Shihuang's Imperial Carriage (110)

I Emperor Qin Shihuang in Profile

Over 2,000 years back, more than 300 supreme rulers exhibited their splendid power and solitary prestige on the historical stage in the feudal society of China. Nevertheless, it was Emperor Qin Shihuang who was the first to establish a unified feudal empire and start with the title "Emperor". He had rare gifts, bold strategy and splendid feats, and exerted a far—reaching and widespread influence in the Chinese history, and therefore proved himself to be an emperor of all.

Emperor Qin Shihuang (259 B.C — — — 210 B.C.), alias Ying Zheng, was born in the closing days of the Warring States Period when the then seven states threw themselves into frequent wars and scrambled for supremacy. When the Qin was at war with the Zhao, his father, Zi Chu, was sent to the Zhao State as a hostage, and lived a destitute and distressful life there. However, Lu Buwei, a man of political and strategic foresight, was doing business in Han Dan of the Zhao State during that period. He considered Zi Chu talented and extraordinary, and made utmost efforts to help him out of the dangerous situation. On the one hand, he offered Zi Chu his pregnant lady, Zhao Ji, who was skilled in singing and dancing. On the other hand, he grudged no money in his endeavour to rescue Zi Chu by lobbying and bribing the officials of the Zhao State. Eventually, Lu Buwei succeeded, and Zi Chu was released, and mounted to the throne back home. Lu Buwei's success devoted a dramatic chapter to the history of rightful succession to the throne in the Qin State. So Zi Chu, once a distress—striken prince, fulfilled his desires to ascend to the throne, and styled himself King Zhuangxiang. After his death, his son, Ying Zheng succeeded him on the throne in the capacity of crown prince.

Ying Zheng, otherwise known as Emperor Qin Shihuang, ascended to the throne at 13, and began to run the imperial government at 22. He proceeded with the policy of making the country rich and building up military power, which had been formulated and implemented by his predecessors since Duke Xiaogong's reign. Meanwhile, he adapted himself to the historical trend, and accelerated the course of annexing the other six states. In this connexion, he recruited wise counsellors and bold soldiers, and accepted Li Si's proposal to conquer the six states and build a unified empire. Later over the years, he dispatched one expedition after another, and staged a unification war against the eastern six states. In the fifteen years from 230 B.C. to 221 B.C., sanguinary battles were fought, and one state after another was conquered. As a result, the first centralized, autocratic feudal empire began to take shape in the Chinese history, and this new prospect put an end to the centuries—old disunion and incessant wars which had originated from the Spring and Autumn Period and the Warring States Period.

Having unified the entire country, Emperor Ying Zheng posed as a man of boundless beneficence, and even considered the Three Emperors and the Five Sovereigns inferior to him. For this reason, he crowned himself with the title "Emperor", and afforded an example as a supreme ruler. Besides, he established himself as the First Emperor, with the hope that his descendants would be the second, the third and even the one hundredth from generation to generation and beyond. But it had never occurred to him that his empire collapsed at all when his son, Emperor Qin Ershi was in power, and that his imperial title would be adopted by later feudal rulers for more than two thousand years. Emperor Qin Shihuang took many political and economic measures to accelerate the social development and consolidate the imperial power. Having accepted Li Si's suggestions, he abolished the enfeoffment system, instituted the prefecture and county system, and secured both political and military power in his own hands.

He enacted well—defined laws and decided everything accordingly. Legal codes served as an important tool for the administration of the whole country. His accomplishments in standardizing written language, currency, weights and measures propelled the economic growth and cultural exchanges, and exerted a favourable and effective influence on the later generations. In addition, Emperor Qin Shihuang ordered the construction of straightways and imperial roads, which made the Qin accessible to these states such as the Yan, Wu, Qi and Chu, and gave an impetus to the transport development and cultural exchanges of that age. He also forced the rank and file to join the separate defence walls of the Warring States Period into what is known as the Great Wall today.

In 210 B.C., or rather at the age of fifty, Emperor Qin Shihuang died from an illness in

◀ Statue of Qin Shi Huang

Pingtai, Shaqiu (in the northwest of Guangzong, Hebei Province) during an inspection tour. Soon after his death, a revolt against the Qin Dynasty swept the whole country, and brought on its complete collapse in 206 B. C.. Up to that time, the Qin Dynasty had existed only for fifteen years. The destruction of the Qin Empire was a tragedy to Emperor Qin Shihuang. In order to intensify his autocratic power and wallow in luxury during his reign, he executed severe penal codes, levied exorbitant taxes, made endless demands on the people, staged one war after another, and ordered large — scaleconstruction works to be built, such as the Great Wall, imperial roads, his mausoleum and A'fang Palace. Almost one — tenth of the total population was forced to serve in the army, which brought a severe hindrance to the development of social production and also a distressful life to the whole populace. His folly of " burning books and burying Confucian scholars alive" played unheard — of havoc with ancient Chinese culture. But inspite of his tyrannical rule, it is this great andcruel historical figure who left behind a massive and grand mausoleum, the first of its kind in China. The mausoleum was creative, magnificent and richly furnished. However, it was an imperial tomb filled with tears and bloodstains as well.

Emperor Qin Shihuang's Mausoleum is located north of the Lishan Mountains in Lintong County in the area of Xi'an. The lofty earth — rammed mound above the tomb, set off by the Lishan Mountains and the glimmering Weihe River, looks imposing, serene and extraordinary. The whole setting allegedly looks like a lotus flower. From a geomantic point of view, the tomb occupies a propitious "lotus — nut" location, hemmed in by the " lotus — petal" peaks of the Lishan Mountains. This enchanting landscape may well present itself before everyone's mental vision.

Emperor Qin Shihuang's Mausoleum, which was modelled after the imperial capital, covers an area of 56. 25 square kilometres.

The lofty earth — rammed mound, rising dramatically from its center, has a grand and sumptuous palace underneath, and two walled enclosures. The inner wall has a circumference of 3,870 meters, and the outer one, 6,210 meters. Each of the walls has four corner towers, and watchtower — crested gates on all four sides. The mausoleum assumes the features of the imperial capital city in layout. The periphery of the city wall is dispersed with the satellite tombs, subordinate burial pits, and other remains that come out in various shapes and sizes. This indicates that the mausoleum just has about everything that was available in the capital city. With the deepening of the archaeological work on the mausoleum over the years, more and yet more relics have been discovered, including ten subordinate burial pits, hundreds of satellite tombs, and the foundation bases for inner and outer city walls, the imperial coffin chamber, the emperor's rest room and the Garden Temple. The historical remains that have been excavated and sorted out include the bronze horse—drawn carriage vault, the building site west of the mausoleum, the stable pit, the rare bird and animal pit, the subordinate tombs for princes and princesses in Shangjiao Village, and the mausoleum builders' cemetery in Zhaobeihu Village. These relics are of great value to the archaeological study of the Qin Dynasty and to our understanding of its social system, culture, customs and material civilization.

There is no doubt that the underground palace below the earth—rammed mound is the most enchanting and mysterious of all the relics. According to The Records of Historians and The Annals of the Han Dynasty, the palace was inlaid with stone, reinforced with bronze, and provided with rare vessels, treasures and furniture. The ceiling was furnished with such astronomical signs as the moon, the sun and constellations. Besides, mechanically—driven mercury rivers and lakes were constructed to represent the earthly world. Exquisite palatial structures were dispersed along the rivers and lakes so that Emperor Qin Shihuang could make a temporary stay there during an inspection tour in the nether world.

Modern science has offered evidence that there is a large quantity of mercury in the underground palace of Emperor Qin Shihuang's Mausoleum. Because of its vertical volatilization, the center of the earth—rammed mound is unusually dominated with strong mercury over an area of 12,000 square meters, and registers a mercury level more than tenfold as high as the surrounding area. This, more or less, indicates that The Records of Historians and The Annals of the Han Dynasty present a faithful and reliable account of Emperor Qin Shihuang's underground palace. Nevertheless, nothing more about the palace is known to us all, for it lies hidden under an area of more than 200,000 square meters. The interior of the palace still remains something in imagination, and an impetrenable mystery to us. We are looking forward to the day when its size, depth, architectural structures and rare treasures will be made known to the whole world.

II A World—Shaking Discov

In the chilly March of 1974, Yang Peiyan, Yang Zhifa and a few other peasants from the inconspicuous Xiyang Village in Lintong County, Shaanxi Province were digging a well when they happened to discover fragments of pottery warriors, and bronze arrowheads, thus opening the door to an underground world wonder. The news swept from Xi'an to Beijing, and stirred up a sensation around the world. In July, 1974, a sortation team which comprised the archaeological experts of Shaanxi Province set out for the site and raised the curtain on the most splendid archaeological project of the century.

In the eyes of these archaeological workers, Emperor Qin Shihuang's Mausoleum was an enchanting sacred complex. They lived in temporary worksheds, and toiled with delight and excitement from morning till night. As a result, they opened one treasure trove after another and a series of underground wonders. Through exploration drilling, Vault II was discovered northeast of Vault I in May, 1976, and again Vault III was located northwest of Vault I in July. The results of archaeological excavations revealed that the site was devoted to vast subordinate burial pits for terra—cotta warriors and horses. Over a total area of more than 20,000 square meters, these pits contained more than 7,000 life—size pottery warriors and horses, over 100 wooden war chariots, and a large variety of exquisite weapons. Emperor Qin Shihuang's Mausoleum has ever since been known as a large world—shaking subterranean military and art museum. As one of the greatest discoveries of this century, the mausoleum has won the title of "the eighth world wonder".

If the discovery of terra—cotta warriors and horses fell on those peasants just out of historica

favoritism, then a series of discoveries that followed, however, owed a great deal to the sweat, toil and wisdom of the archaeological workers. With the strong desires to discover the traces and wonders of the remote antiquity, a batch of archaeologists tracked in the fields and gullies around the mausoleum, drilled tens upon thousands of holes here and there, and as a result, discovered one underground treasure—trove after another. In October, 1976, the satellite tombs for princes and princesses in Shangjiao Village were discovered and partly excavated. In March, 1977, the sites of Emperor Qin Shihuang's burial chamber and rest—house were discovered, and in July, the pit for pottery birds and animals was found around the mausoleum. From 1979 to 1980, the mausoleum builders' cemetery in Zhaobeihu Village, and the stable pit were discovered, and sorted out on a partial basis. On a hot day of September, 1978, the archaeological workers were immersed in exploration drilling, when they lifted a bubble—shaped golden ornament from the depth of seven or eight meters below the ground. The experts on the exploration team couldn't hold their excited feelings after they had accepted it as a rare ornament on the bronze horse, and determined there was another trove of relics underground. Upon the approval of the state government, excavations were undertaken at the site on November 5, 1980. Twenty—eight days later, a bronze horse—drawn chariot or a bronze gem in a class by itself, that had existed underground for more than two thousand years was brought to light. The news spread like wildfire, and stirred up a sensation all over the world, and produced a series of miraculous effects. Almost all of a sudden, visitors came in uninterrupted crowds, and the excavation site was closely surrounded. Emperor Qin Shihuang's Mausoleum has ever since remained an attraction to the entire world. Over the years, all the terra — cotta army vaults and the relevant relics have been housed and exhibited to visitors from different parts of the world. On October 1, 1979, Vault I was formally opened to the public. On October 1, 1983, Horse — drawn Carriage II was restored and openly exhibited. On May 1, 1988, Horse—drawn Carriage I was displayed to the public. On September 27, 1989, Terra—cotta Army Vault III was opened to visitors. Vault II was formally excavated on March 1, 1994, and will be exhibited to the public this coming October. Over the past ten years, Emperor Qin Shihuang's Terra — cotta Army Museum has received more than twenty — six million domestic visitors, two million foreign guests and one thousand government officials. In May, 1976, Sigaporean Premier Lee Kuan Yew visited the museum with delight, and expressed his admiration by writing down the words "A wonder of the world and a pride of the nation". In September, 1978, French Premier Jacques Chirac explicitly called it " the eighth world wonder". Later, more than 70 heads of state, including the U.S. President Nixon and Reagan, Japanese Prime Minister Ohira Masayoshi, the UK Queen Elizabeth, Korean Chairman Kim Ill Sung and German Premier Cole, all came to visit Emperor Qin Shihuang's Mausoleum and left behind their words of admiration and high praise in multiple written languages.

III A Valiant Army in Full Battle Array

There are three terra—cotta army vaults about 1,500 meters from Emperor Qin Shihuang's Mausoleum. They are numbered Vault I, Vault II and Vault III in order of discovery. Each vault is a unit by itself, but forms an integral whole with the other two. These separate vaults constitute a compact military camp, which symbolically refers to the Night Guards Army formerly stationed in the capital city. More than 7,000 pottery soldiers are well—armed with armour and weapons, hundreds of battle steeds are pawing the ground restlessly. This scene vividly reflects the fact that the Qin Empire had a military force of more than one million armoured warriors, one thousand battle chariots, and ten thousand cavalrymen. The entire army seems to be in full battle array and ready for combat. Vault I is the principal component of the entire military camp. It comes out in an oblong shape, 230 meters from east to west and 62 meters from north to south, and covers a total area of 14,260 square meters. The largest of all in size, the vault contains an oblong battle formation with more than 600 pottery infantrymen and horses, and over 40 war chariots. The formation consists of four parts: the van, the body, the flank and the rear. The van which is located in the extreme front of the vault comprises the first three rows of pottery soldiers in perfect alignment, with a total number of 204. The vanguards wear tressed hair, and reveal putty—clad legs. Armed with strong bows and stiff crossbows, they look valiant, skilful in shooting, and as irresistible as sharp—pointed swords. Except for the van, Vault I is partitioned into eleven corridors, all in an east—west direction. Along these corridors stand thirty—eight columns of armoured, putty—clad infantry-

men that alternate with war chariots. They carry long—handled weapons such as spears, dagger—axes lances and halberds, and a limited number of bows and crossbows. These heavy—armoured pottery warriors and the war chariots constitute the main body of the battle formation, and exhibit an unbreakable and all—conquering force. There is a row of warrior figures along the northern and southern rims of the vault respectively. One row is facing north; the other is facing south. The northern row is the left flank; the southern one, the right flank. Their task is to defend against enemy attack from the flanks. At the rear of the battle formation, there is a row of warrior figures facing west and backing against the main force. They serve as the rear of the battle formation, and defend against enemy attack from the back.

Vault II is located about 20 meters north of the eastern end of Vault I. The vault is shaped like a T—square on the horizontal plane. With a length of 124 meters from east to west and a width of 98 meters from north to south, it covers a total area of 6,000 square meters. The results of exploration drilling and test excavations have revealed that Vault II is estimated to contain a composite T—shaped battle formation of infantrymen, cavalrymen, light chariots and other arms of the services. Statistically, the vault comprises 89 wooden chariots, and 1,300 pottery warriors and horses, including 350 chariot horses, 100 saddled horses and 900 warriors of every description. Actually, this battle formation, more or less, serves as the flank, as compared with the principal force in Vault I, and ranks high in the scales of sudden attack. It is a combination of four individual battle arrays. The first array is located in the extreme

front of the T—shaped formation. It is composed of 230 crossbow archers altogether. About 160 heavy—armoured kneeling archers in a column of eights are positioned in the center, and an additional 170 robe—clad standing archers are arranged in ring array. So when it comes to enemy assault, dripping showers of arrows can be shot from two different positions alternately to prevent the enemy from approaching. The second array lies on the right side of the T—shaped formation. It consists of 64 war chariots, and each of them is provided with a charioteer, three chariot warriors and two armoured ones. Because of their quick movement and shock action, the chariot warriors frightened and wiped out the enemy in the then battlefields. The third array is centered in the T—shaped formation. In fact, it is a composite column array that takes war chariots, infantrymen and cavalrymen as a combined whole. The array is predominated by 19 war chariots, with 260 infantrymen as the auxiliary force and with 8 cavalrymen as the rear. The fourth one is the cavalrymen's array located on the left side of the T—shaped battle formation. The array proper is predominated by 108 cavalrymen, and supported by 6 war chariots. They are tall and robust. They wear fur hats and leather boots, and reveal armoured chests. Bow in one hand, and rein in the other, they look swift, natural and unrestrained. The battle steeds are plump and sturdy, and each of them has a saddle with a saddle cloth on the back. It can be well imagined that these cavalrymen are lightning — quick, whirlwind — swift and so powerful as to break into the enemy ranks, once they thrust themselves into a battle.

Vault III is located 25 meters north of the western end of Vault I, and 120 meters west of Vault II. The vault is a concave polygon on the horizontal plane. Its total area is no more than 500 square meters. It is the smallest of the three, and has the smallest number of pottery warriors. The relics excavated from the vault include 66 pottery warriors, 4 chariot horses and a wooden war chariot. The pottery warriors are arranged not in battle array, but along the walls of two wing—rooms. They stand face to face in two rows, each with a pointed bronze pole in hand. Obviously, they are a guards regiment to defend the headquarters. Also unearthed from the vault are deer—horns and animal bones, mostly probably left behind from the ancient sacrificial rites and war prayers. Judging from all these phenomena, Vault III is different from the other two vaults in layout, and it is most likely the seat of what was known as a military command in ancient times.

As an integral miniature of battle formations, these vaults vividly exhibit the scene of the Qin army's rattling chariots, neighing horses, valiant warriors and heavily — guarded headquarters, and represent the mighty military power of the Qin Empire that dates 2,000 years back. Besides, they constitute a vivid and direct—visual battle formation map. They provide us with telling and concrete examples to show the arms of the services, battle formation and weapon allocation, strategy and tactics of the ancient times. This miniature gives an ocular reflection of the battle—formation principles that the strategists of the past ages highly valued, such as " The blade—point of a sword must be sharp, its blade must be thin, and its body must be strong. ", " If the front and the rear take concerted action and never vacillate, then the enemy is destined to retreat in defeat. ", and " Use war chariots on a flatland, cavalrymen in a dangerous situation, and crossbows at a strategic pass. " (Sun Bin's Strategy and Tactics). No wonder that these battle—formation vaults have been accepted as a dimensional book on the art of war.

IV A Statue Complex of High Artistic Value

If there were remarkable achievements in the history of statue art in ancient China, then the statue complex of Emperor Qin Shihuang's terra—cotta warriors and horses, without doubt, were the crest of those accomplishments. The pottery warriors were full of might and splendour, and added a shining page to the history of Oriental statue art.

The statue complex subordinate to Emperor Qin Shihuang's Mausoleum reflects a wide range of artistic achievements. In the first place, it affords an imposing and unprecedented macroscopic view. The warrior figures are tall and large, mighty and valiant. Anyone who has ever been here could not dismiss them from their minds for a long time. More than 7,000 terra—cotta warriors and horses are arrayed over an area of several 10,000 square meters. Generals, soldiers, horses and chariots, in rows and columns, constitute a powerful and valiant army which would blot out the vast sky, and conquer rivers and mountains by order. An average warrior figure ranges in height from 1.8 meters to a maximum of 2 meters, and has a large and strong build. An average horse figure is life—size, 2 meters long and 1.7 meters tall. These warrior and horse figures rank first both in number and in height among all the pottery figures of the past ages that have been unearthed in China up till now.

Realistic depiction features the terra—cotta warriors and horses of the Qin Dynasty. Judging from the one thousand pottery warriors and horses unearthed so far, the statue complex of the Qin Dynasty is basically realistic in style, with apparent characteristics of real images and sketches from life. The terra—cotta warriors and horses are used as the motif of artistic creation. Their images are vivid and lifelike, accurate and well—proportioned, as if each and every pottery warrior and horse was modelled after a prototype. The terra—cotta horses display the mien of "galloping willingly without being whipped", with upright and square heads, big noses, wide mouths, fat hips and round waists, and fully—grown muscles, with the eyes like dangling bells, the ears like sharpened bamboo, the forelegs like pillars and the hind legs like bows. The terra—cotta figures are divided into three major classes according to their martial status: general figures, military official figures and warrior figures. Different figures wear different dresses and personal adornments, and assume different manners and postures. The general figures are tall and strong. They wear double long—sleeved jackets, colorful suits of fish—scale armour around the shoulders, brown caps on their heads, and square—mouth pointed shoes. All these demonstrate their poise and refinement in a laudable tolerant spirit. The military official figures generally wear long jackets, suits of armour around the shoulders, and long caps, and exhibit a standing posture with weapons in hand, thus displaying their mighty masculine spirit of having fought countless battles and facing death unflinchingly. The warrior figures are moulded, and posed according to the arms of services. The kneeling crossbow warriors shoot with their right knees on the ground and both hands setting crossbows. The standing crossbow warriors shoot with their left feet half a step forward. Their two feet take the shape of the letter T, with the left legs arched and the right legs back—stretched, and with the left arms out—stretched and the right arms folded in front of the chests, setting their crossbows and getting ready to shoot. All of them look quite natural and life—like. The most picturesque and vivid touch lies in the portrait of facial expressions, so much so that no "twins" can be found among all the terra—cotta figures. Some wear heavy eyebrows, have big eyes, high nose—bridges and whiskers, and manifest a sanguine disposition. Some look solemn and serious with long faces and heavy moustaches. Some face others with frowning brows and angry eyes, so indignant that they are ready to roar. Some have long faces and light brows, with their lips tightly closed and their eyes looking down, and seem to be lost in thought. Some have delicate features, crack a slight smile, and look naive and lively. Every face in a different expression serves as the man's curriculum vitae, in which you could read his nationality, age, birthplace and even his temperament. No wonder some people could recognize farmers from the Central Shaanxi Plains, boys from Sichuan as well as herdsmen from the northern grassland, out of so many terra—cotta warriors.

Coloured drawing is one of the outstanding features of these pottery figures. The original beautiful colours on the clay warriors and horses have peeled off, owing to the fire disaster in history and the erosion of underground water and soil in the past two thousand years. Those colours such as red, green, blue, white, black and yellow are roughly discernible on a portion of pottery warriors and horses. It is not difficult to imagine how brilliant and grand the terra—cotta army vault looked when first built. In the process of coloured decoration, special attention was paid to the treatment of clothing and adornments, with the best concentration on the faces of the terra—cotta warriors. The Qin artists placed much stress on the portrait of facial expressions in the modelling of pottery figures, and proved very calculating in the formation of foreheads, brows, nose—bridges, chins, cheeks and hair. The dividing lines between rise and fall on the faces were portrayed through appropriate exaggeration, for example, the spaces between the eyebrows, lips and beards. When the colours were applied, these parts looked natural and smooth, and the five sense organs stood out without being ... us forming a unique and perfect artistic combination between coloured drawings and pottery statues. There were at least three layers in the colours on the faces: raw lacquer, pink or other colours, and light white. The think layers of colours symbolize the splendour of the skin and muscles. In the depiction of eyes, which was in the minutest details, the black pupillas and the yellowish pupils were distinguished with colours, embodying the traditional style of putting in the pupils of the eyes in Chinese sculpture and drawings.

In the creation of the Qin figures, sculpture and moulding were combined, with sculpture as the main mode, and various traditional skills as auxiliary techniques such as pushing, moulding, sticking, carving, and painting. The body parts were modelled with strips of mud one layer upon another, and then robes or suits of armour were carved, stuck or moulded. The modeling of the heads was more complicated, with the rough—casts moulded first, the back heads piled and sculptured with ears and ready—made buns stuck to one side of the head, and with other detailed parts such as eyes, brows, mouths and beards depicted so as to reveal the different dispositions of the concrete objects. The skills in baking of the Qin figures were unique and super. According to the tests and analysis, the figures were baked in the temperatures between 950 to 1050 degrees centigrade, reaching the level of pure blue flames, which cannot be reached even today in the tests, a level which defies all comparison.

The art of sculpture of the Qin figures was the outstanding creation of the ancient Chinese people, a splendid jewel dedicated to the treasure house of human civilization.

V The Exquisite Weaponry of the Qin Dynasty

All the figures of warriors were equipped with real bronze weapons. Up to now nearly 40, 000 weapons in over a dozen categories have been unearthed from one tenth of the whole Qin pits of terra—cotta army, such as swords, spears, crossbows, bronze hooks and arrows, including almost all the weapons which had equipped the army of the Qin Dynasty. The majority of the weapons were the ones for shooting. Twenty—two bronze swords were unearthed in a corner at the east end. These swords, which are still shining and sharp as before, remind people of the line from Li Bai's poem that " The light of the sword shines the sky, and it becomes blue itself. " The handles of Qin weapons were longer, the longest being 3.82

metres, made of wood or bamboo, bound with strings and painted with lacquer. There are inscriptions carved on many weapons, mainly the names of officials or workers, which serve as valuable data for the studies of the history of ancient weapons, the history of ancient system of the administration of workers as well as the changes of Chinese characters.

All the weapons were cast pieces and then they were processed in a refined and scientific way, so that they were well—shaped with sharp blades. The precision in processing is almost incredible. The accuracy in the making of the arrowheads is similar to that of the modern bullets, an excellence which is enough to make people thumb the table and shout " Brave! "

On the surface of the bronze weapons, there is a layer of oxide coating with chromic salts, which is as thick as 10 microns with very fine effects of anti—rust and anti—corrosion. That is why those weapons are still shining when the dust was got rid of from their surfaces after having been buried for over two thousand years. It has to be admitted that it is a wonder since the European and American countries mastered the anti—rust techniques only in modern times. Irregular decorative patterns were found on the surface of the weapons, which remain a mystery even today, for they were not cast or carved. Some people assumed they might have been made through the treatment of vulcanization. Whatever might be the method, it played an important role in the history of China's metallurgical manufacture.

Among the alloys used for the Qin weapons unearthed in the pits, the content of tin was increased apparently. According to the tests of the bronze sword, the content of bronze accounts for 71———74. 6%, and that of tin 21. 38——— 31%. The content of bronze in spears makes up 69. 62%, and that of tin 30. 38%. Therefore, it might be concluded that the proportioning of bronze and alloys before and after the Qin dynasty were more scientific and standardized. The Qin Empire made brilliant achievements in metallurgical manufacture.

VI Emperor Qin Shihuang's Imperial Carriage

There seems to be no denying the magnificence of ancient imperial carriages. In the feudal dynasties of past ages, much was written about the " imperial carriage and formal gowns system ". Nevertheless, none of the original imperial carriages were preserved until modern times, and their splendour and sumptuousness existed only in the sea of human imagination. When it came to the 1980's, the archaeologists, probably out of historical favouritism, discovered a subordinate burial vault twenty meters west of Emperor Qin Shihuang's Maosuleum, and excavated two exquisite and painted bronze horse — drawn carriages. These two imperial carriages have ever since been exhibited to the general public.

The vault, 50 meters in length and in width, amounts to a total area of 3,025 square meters. The vault contains five pits, with a pair of imperial carriages in each. In the year of 1980, one of the pits was excavated, and two painted bronze horse — drawn carriages were unearthed. Each of the carriages is four — wheeled and single — shafted, and complete with four horses and a pottery imperial driver. They are one meter in height, and half the size of the original, but 2.25 and 3.17 meters in length respectively. They are two large bronze complexes that comprise more than 6,000 complicated parts which range in weight from one to another. Each bronze horse weighs over 200 kilograms, but somedecorative articles are less than 50 grams. These parts were finely moulded and exquisitely put together. Both warrior and horse figures were vividly depicted, and the decorative articles were meticulously wrought. The carriages were painted in colors all over. They were accepted as excellent examples in the history of bronze moulding. Professor Su Bai, a well—renowned archaeologist, rated them as the "crest of bronze—

wares".

These two bronze horse — drawn carriages form a well — matched pair. The front one, also known as the " high carriage ", takes an oblong shape. It is 48.5 c.m. long and 74 c.m. wide. It is enclosed with rails on three sides, and its back is wide open. The carriage is covered with a canopy, under which there is a standing high — ranking driver. Both the interior and exterior are fitted with exquisite bronze crossbows, arrowheads and shields. The back one, also called " security carriage " has a front chamber and a back chamber. In the front chamber there is a kneeling high—ranking imperial driver. The rear chamber is for his master to sit in. It is 88 c.m. long and 78 c.m. wide. It is tightly closed, with a door at the back, and a canopy on top.

According to the results of archaeological research, the ten carriages in five pairs, including the above — mentioned two ones were part of the carriage fleet that accompanied Emperor Qin Shihuang on his inspection tour. The horse—drawn carriage pits represent the imperial carriage barn. It was an important part of 2 his political life to make an inspection tour by carriage. He specially instituted the " Guards — of — Honor System ", which classified his carriages into three broad categories: large, medium and small. The large carriage was used on important occasions, and followed by eighty—one subordinate carriages.

The medium carriage had three subordinate carriages after it. The small carriage was accompanied by nine subordinate carriages. The ten carriages in these two pits were generally accepted as the subordinate carriages accompanying the medium carriage. They were called " subordinate carriages in five pairs ", including five "security carriages " and five " high carriages ". They fell into

the common category. The two imperial carriage that have been unearthed are exhibited to the public in the Museum of Emperor Qin Shihuang's Mausoleum. In the presence of these carriages, we can fully imagine how majestic and dignified Emperor Qin Shihuang was on his inspection tour. No wonder Liu Bang, the first emperor of the Western Han Dynasty sighed out with emotion, "This is what a gentleman should be !" when he saw a fleet of splendid carriages followed Emperor Qin Shihuang on an inspection tour.

These bronze carriages are realistic works of art, characterized by exquisite workmanship, accurate moulding and strict structural proportion. They may well be regarded as models of ancient bronze carriages. Meticulously portrayed in detailed parts, they are faithful to the original both in form and in character. The braided leather, reins and bridles, hair and fabrics are all true to life. The carriages, together with the terra—cotta warriors and horses have almost caused a revolution in man's inherent understanding of ancient Chinese statue art. In fact, they have been accepted as the gems of Chinese formative arts.

The imperial drivers are highly representative of the bronze carriages in terms of moulding, and serve as excellent examples of ancient formative arts. Each work of art gives a vivid and accurate depiction of a high—ranking imperial official, and places much stress on the creation of his romantic

charm and striking personality. The figure looks respectful, cautious and discreet. The smile in the eyes and on the lips suggests that he is fully satisfied with his position as an imperial official. He wears a long—sleeved jacket with a kummerbund, a brown hat and a sword around the waist, all of which are signs of his official status. His characteristic action of grasping reins and bridles which co — ordinates with his facial expression is exquisitely depicted that it reflects a high level of artistic attainments. The eight horses are also finely moulded. They look muscular and full of energy. Their ears stand upright like sharpened bamboo, their eyes are as large as two hanging bells, and their heads are high up in the air. All these features reflect their strength and alertness.

The bronze carriages are excellent examples of colored drawing and decoration. They are decorated with more than 4,000 gold and silver structural members. For example, Carriage II is exquisitely adorned with 737 gold members and 983 silver ones. These adornments are mainly found in eye—catching places and on the horse gear, including silver linchpin, silver canopy tips, gold and silver hatlers, gold and silver reins. The entire carriage radiates with rays of gold and silver, and reveals the owner's dignity and majestic power.

The bronze carriages are painted with decorative designs in a myriad of colors, including vermilion, pink, green, light green, jade green, dark

blue, light blue, black and brown. The designs and patterns are fine and exquisite, and exhibit the designer's great skill in creating the style of the bronze carriages. In spite of their large size, complicated construction and tremendous painting work, the carriages are finely decorated with colorful designs and patterns which assume the same style, but reflect numerous changes. All these give an excellent reflection of the designer's high artistic attainments.

The decorative designs and patterns on the bronze carriages amount to more than one hundred, within ten broad categories. However, the carriages are dominated phoenix and dragon patterns, rhombus patterns, cloud patterns, and geometric patterns. These decorative designs are relatively concentrated. Their arrangement is subject to position and appropriacy. The patterns are flexibly painted, sequentially distributed and well co—ordinated. The variegated patterns constitute an integral whole, and assume the distinctive features of colored drawing or decoration.

The bronze carriages exhibit a high level of metallurgical casting, junction and assembly of complicated parts in the Qin Dynasty. Despite of their large sizes, complicated shapes, and arc and right angles, the large castings of the bronze carriages are moulded up to strict specifications. Take

Carriage II for example, its canopy is a large dome — shaped casting piece, which ranges in width from one to four millimetres. The canopy fastener is typically a super—long casting piece, with a diameter of six millimetres, and a length of five meters. It has been accepted as the queen of super—long and thin bronze castings moulded in ancient China. The casting and moulding of the canopy and its fastener require sophisticated techniques of proportioning bronze and alloys. The results of modern scientific tests have revealed that these casting pieces were exquisitely moulded. The

bronze carriages were also treated with shrin kon techniques. All of these techniques reflect that the Qin Empire was experienced in the casting and moulding of bronze—wares. The machining, junction and assembly techniques exhibited by the bronze chariages are also eye—catching and amazing. Statistically, the two carriages comprise more than 7,000 spare parts, 7,500 mouthpieces, 1,000 welded joints and 300 design joints. Without advanced machining, assembly and junction techniques, so many parts and components could not have been combined into a whole carriage. These wonderful and sophisticated techniques may well have added a shining page to the metal history of China and the whole world.

▲ (Full View of) Mausloeum of Qin Shi Huang

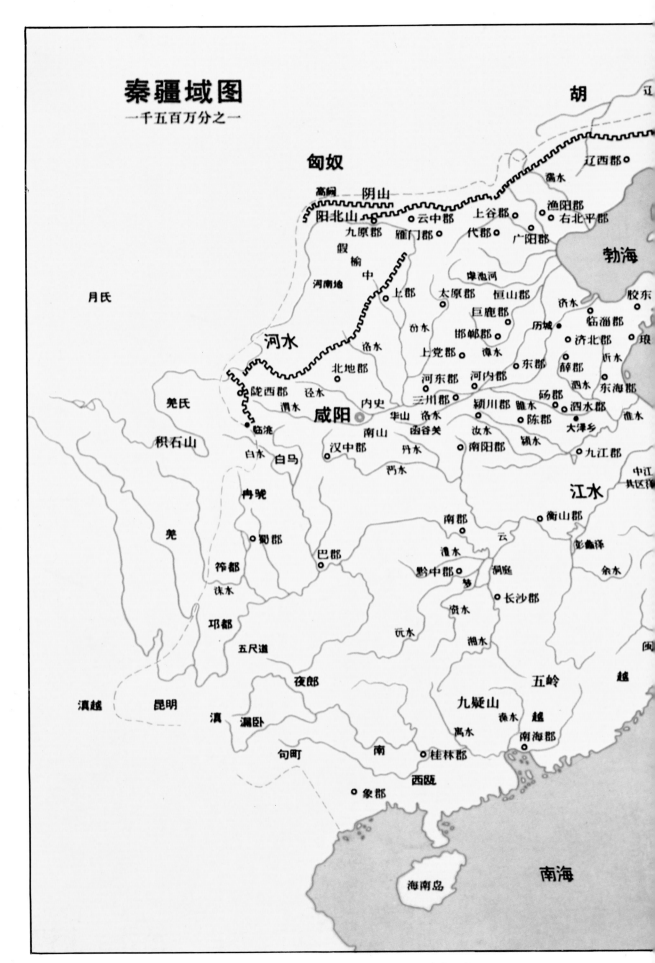

秦疆域图

一千五百万分之一

胡

匈奴

辽西郡

濡水

阴山

高阙

阳北山

云中郡

渔阳郡

右北平郡

九原郡

雁门郡

代郡

上谷郡

广阳郡

勃海

月氏

假榆中

摩池河

太原郡

恒山郡

济水

胶东

河水

河南地

上郡

巨鹿郡

临淄郡

历城

济北郡

琅

汾水

邯郸郡

羌氏

陇西郡

泾水

北地郡

洛水

上党郡

漳水

东郡

薛郡

泗水

东海郡

积石山

渭水

内史

河东郡

河内郡

三川郡

砀郡

泗水郡

雎水

陈郡

淮

白水

临洮

咸阳

华山

南山

函谷关

颍川郡

汝水

大泽乡

白马

汉中郡

丹水

南阳郡

颍水

九江郡

羌

冉駹

沔水

江水

中江其区稽

南郡

衡山郡

蜀郡

云

彭蠡泽

筰都

巴郡

黔中郡

洞庭

余水

闽

汶水

梦

长沙郡

邛都

五尺道

沅水

岭水

湘水

五岭

越

滇越

昆明

夜郎

滇

漏卧

九疑山

溱水

越

羌

句町

离水

南

桂林郡

南海郡

西瓯

象郡

海南岛

南海

▲ Map on Domain of Qin Dynasty

沃
沮

余憒

东海

台湾岛

图   例

⊙   咸阳   都城
○   陈郡   郡级驻地
●   大泽乡   其他居民地
— — — —   政权部族界

▼ A Terra-Cotta Figure Sitting on Knees

▼ Tiger-Shaped Tally with Charactfers of "杜"(Du)

▼ Bronze Coin with the Characters of "Banliang" of Qin Dynasty

▲Pottery Water Pipe

赵背后

董家村

秦始皇陵布局平面图

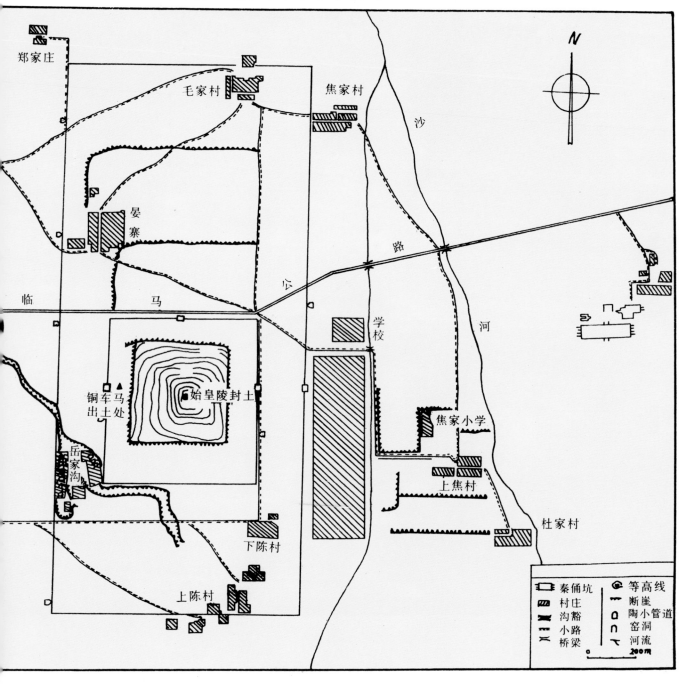

▲ Sketch Map on the Construction of Ground of the Mausoleum of Qin Shi Huang

◀ An Eave Tile of Qin Dynasty

▼ An Eave File of Unusual Size

A World-Sha

King Discovery

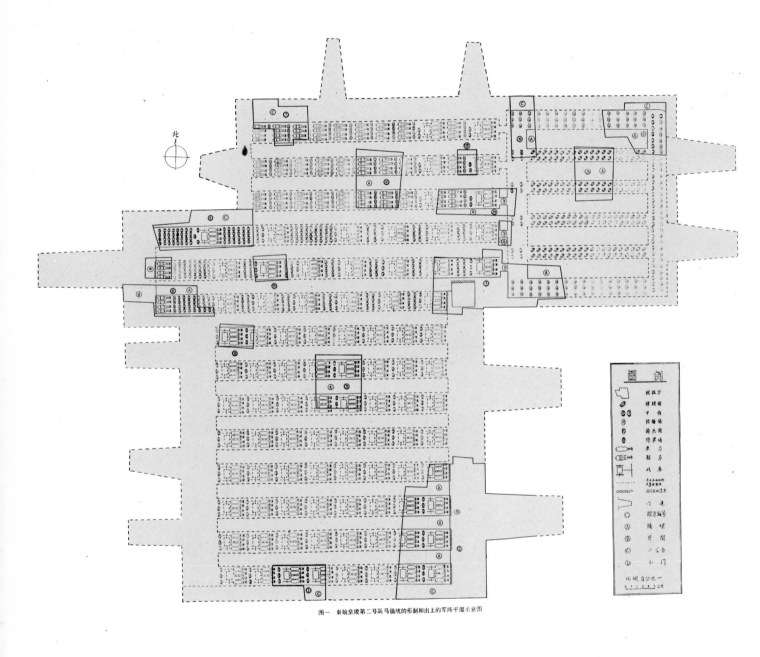

图一　秦始皇陵第二号兵马俑坑的形制和出土的军阵平面示意图

▲ Excavation of No. 2 Pit

Exterior of No. 3 Pit

二層臺
FRAMEWORK

車馬房
STABLE

隔墙
PARTITION WALL

戰車遺跡
THE HISTORICAL REMAINS
OF THE WAR CHARIOT

廊

北厢房
THE NORTHERN
CHAMBER

门楣遗迹
THE HISTORICAL REMAINS OF
TEH LINTEL OVER THE DOOR

鹿甬遗迹
THE HISTORICAL REMAINS
OF THE DEERHORN

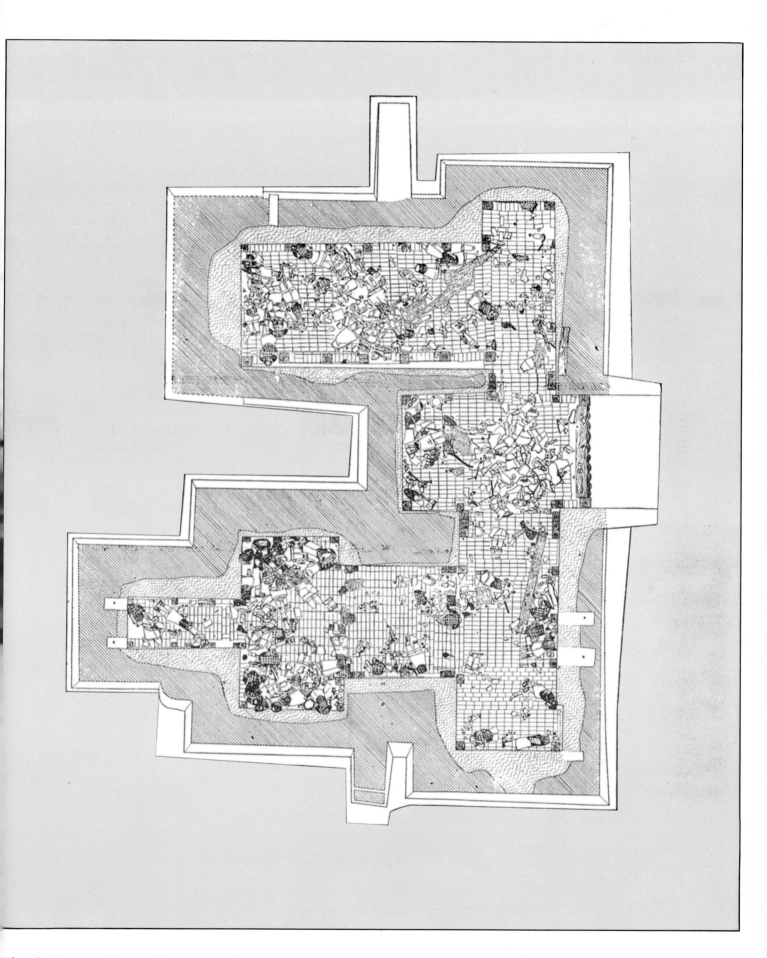

Sketch Map on Military Dispostions of No. 3 Pit

A Mighty Army in Full Battle Array

▼ Part of Varguard of the Battle Array of No. 1 Pit

▲ Full View of No. 1 Pit

▲ Part of No. 1 Pit

▼ Archaeologists at Work in No. 1 pit

▲ Part of No. 3 Pit

◀ A Terra-Cotta Charioteer

Repaired Chariot and Charioteer

▲ A Terra-Cotta Horse

◀Vanguard of the Battle Array of No. 1 Pit

▲ A View of the Battle Array of No. 1 Pit

▲ A Terra-Cotta General

▲ A Terra-Cotta Standing Crossbowman

▲ Terra-Cotta Warriors in Battle Tunics

▲ A Terra-Cotta Armoured Warrior

▼ A Terra-Cotta Cavalry man and a Terra-Cotta Saddled horses

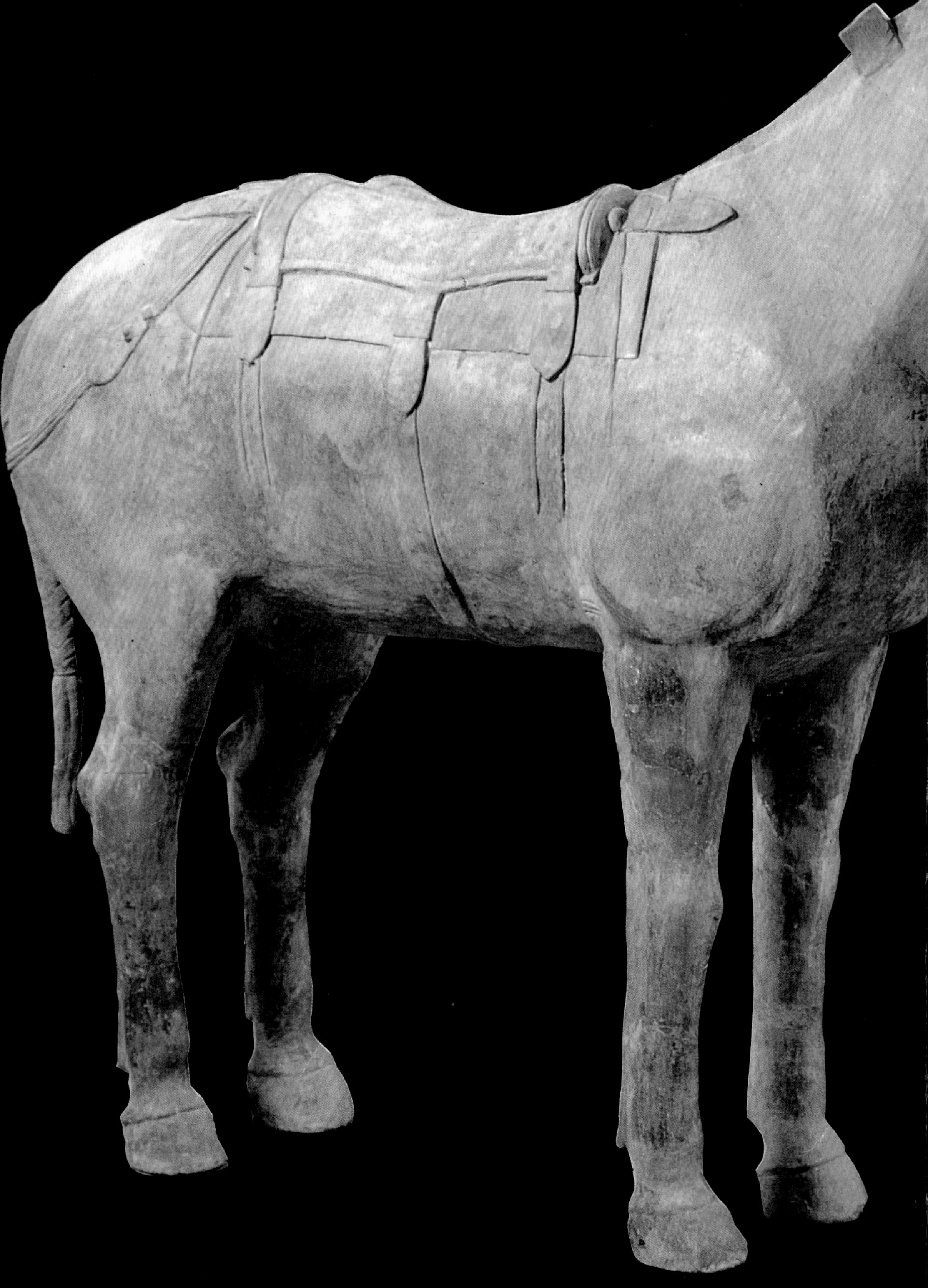

▲ A Terra-Cotta Kneeling Archer

▲ A Terra-Cotta Kneeling Archer (Back View)

▲ A Terra-Cotta Horse

A Statue Complex of High Artistic Value

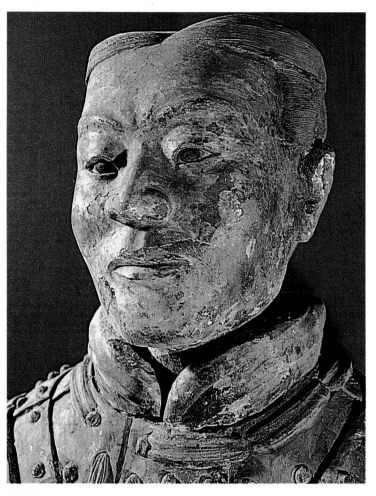

▲ Close-up of the Heads of Terra-Cotta Warrior

Standing Terra-Cotta
Office in Armous

96

▼ Colour Painting on the body of Terra-Cotta Figure

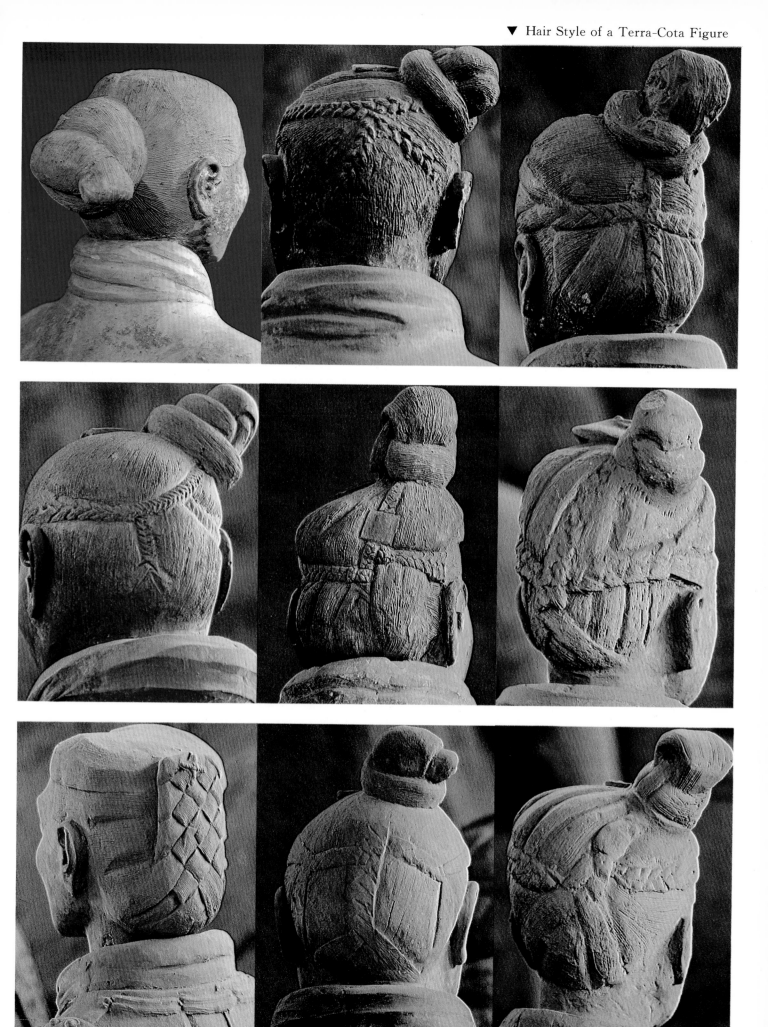

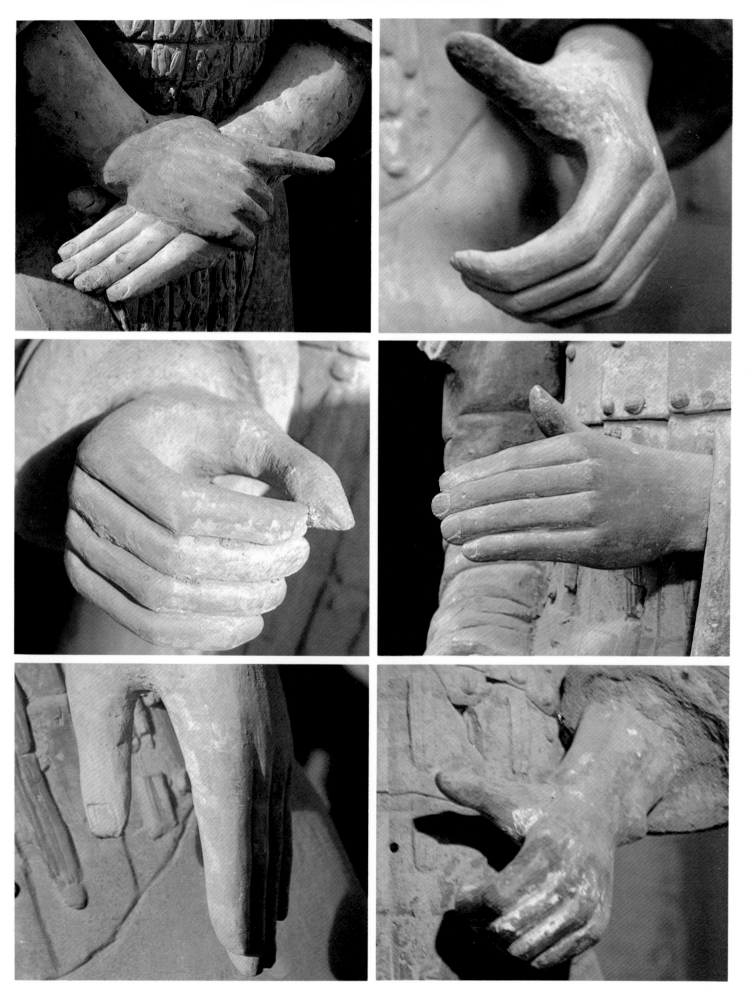

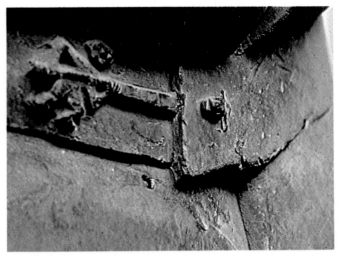

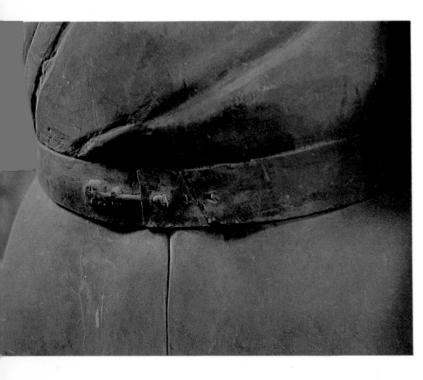

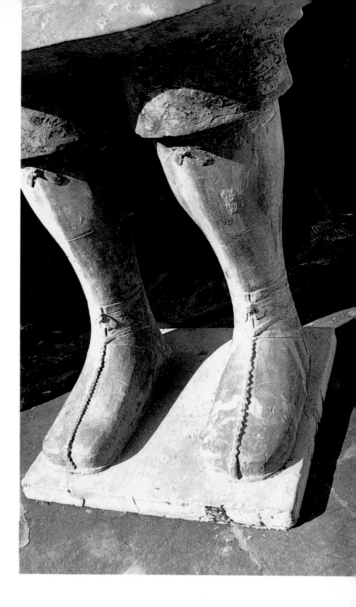

▲ Veried Standing Postures

▲ Patterns Back on the Shoes of Kneeling Archer

The Exquisite Weaponry
of the Qin Dynasty

▼bronze Swordedge—Spear

▼ Bronze Arrow—heads

 Bronze Sword ▶

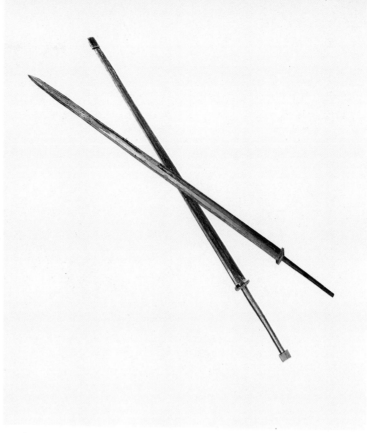

▲ Bronze Halberds

▲ Bronze Crossbow Meohanism

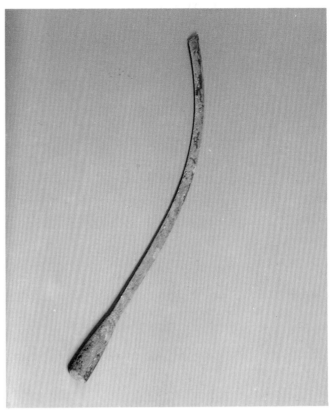

▲ Scimitars（Wugu）

108   ▲ Bronze Arrow—heads

Duplicated Model of
Bronze Crossbow ▶

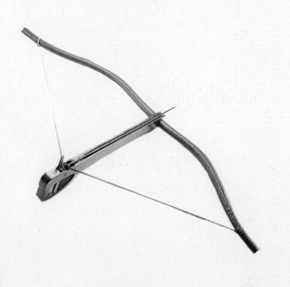

Bronze Bamboo
▼ Weapens

Emperor Qin Shihuang's Imperial Carriage

▲ Restored No. 1 Bronze Chariot

▲ Restorde No. 2 Bronze Chariot

Bronze Pot ▶

▼ Righr Side—Horse

◀ Borse Hard—Net

Gold and Silver
Ornaments on the
Umbrella stick of ▶
No. 1 Chariot

▼ A Wheel in Chariot

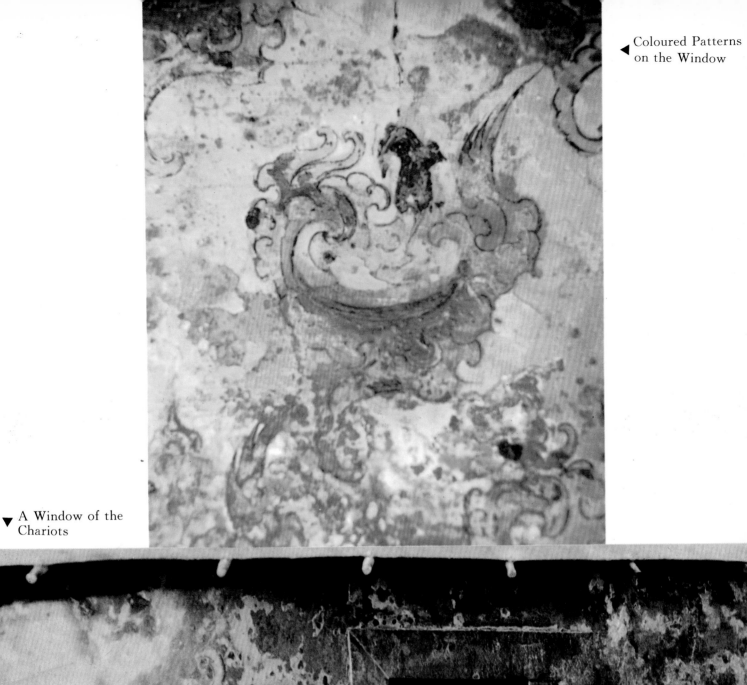

Coloured Patterns
on the Window

A Window of the
Chariots

▲ Gold and Silver Head—Net of a Horse

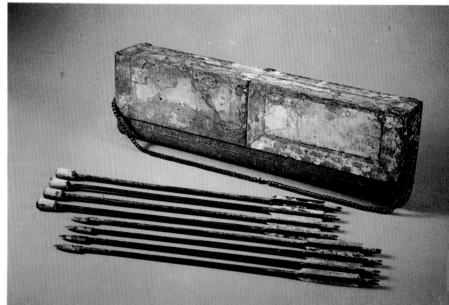

A Bronze Shield in
Coloured Painting ▶

122

▲Righr Side—Horse

Bronze bell

UNITED NATIONS EDUCATIONAL,
SCIENTIFIC AND
CULTURAL ORGANIZATION

CONVENTION CONCERNING
THE PROTECTION OF THE WORLD
CULTURAL AND NATURAL
HERITAGE

The World Heritage Committee
has inscribed

The Mausoleum of the First Qin Emperor

on the World Heritage List

Inscription on this List confirms the exceptional
and universal value of a cultural or
natural site which requires protection for the benefit
of all humanity

DATE OF INSCRIPTION
11 December 1987

DIRECTOR-GENERAL
OF UNESCO

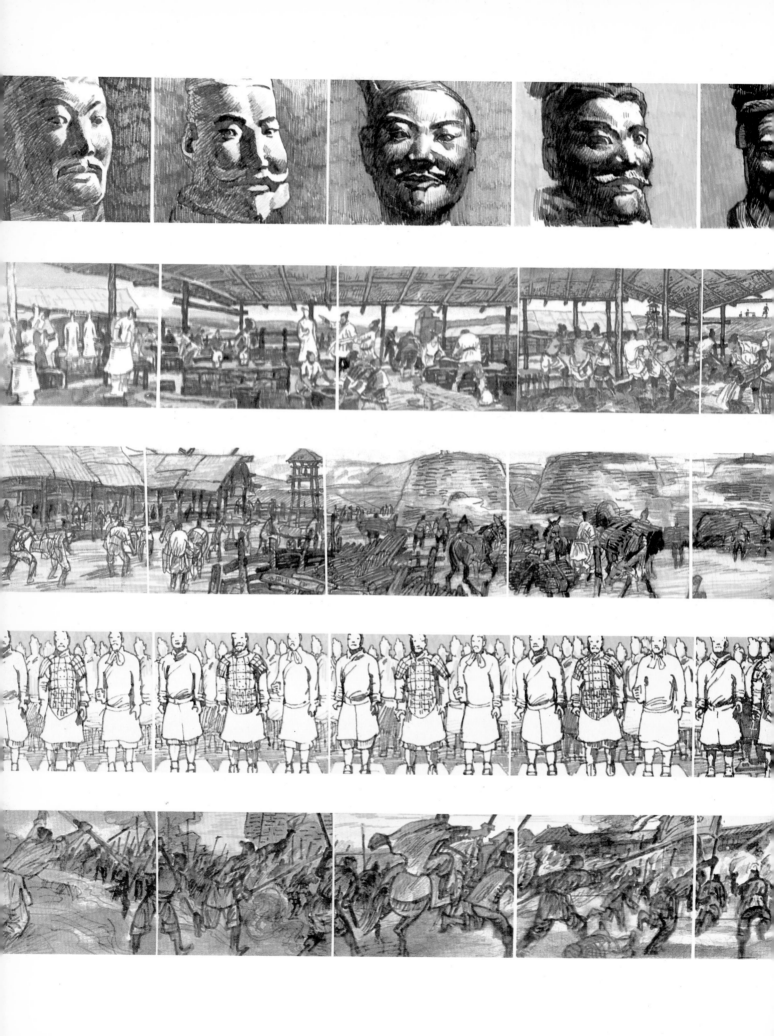

Emperor Qin Shihuang's Eternal Terra-cotta Warriors and Horses

——A Mighty and Valiant Underground Army Over 2,200 Years Back

Managing editor:Li Bing-wu

Deputy managing editor:Zhang Zhong-li;Hei Feng

Planner:Zhang Hui

Photographer:Hei Feng   Qiu Zi-yu   Guo You-min

          Luo Zhong-min   Gao Yu-ying

Translator:Li Rui-lin

Responsible editor:Ge Wei

Cover designer:Shi Wen-bo

Graphic designer:Zhang Yan   Zhang Hui

❋❋❋❋❋❋❋❋❋❋❋❋❋❋❋❋❋❋❋❋❋❋❋❋❋❋❋

Compiled by Shaanxi Historical Relics Bureau

Published by Shaanxi Sanqin Publishing House

Printed by Xi'an No. 2 Printing House

Book xize:998×1194 mm/16 mo.   Sheet No:8

First published and printed in May,1994

Total impression:1—5,000

ISBN 7—80546—798—6/K · 228
0010000